MILITARY AIRCRAFT OF EASTERN EUROPE
2) BOMBERS & ATTACK AIRCRAFT

Piotr Butowski

PUBLICATIONS COMPANY

603-609 Castle Peak Road
Kong Nam Industrial Building
10/F, B1, Tsuen Wan
New Territories, Hong Kong

We welcome authors who can help expand our range of books. If you would like to submit material, please feel free to contact us.

We are always on the look-out for new, unpublished photos for this series. If you have photos or slides or information you feel may be useful to future volumes, please send them to us for possible future publication. Full photo credits will be given upon publication.

ISBN 962-361-035-1
Printed in Hong Kong

Front Cover

MiG-27K armed with a Kh-31P anti-radiation missile. (Piotr Butowski)

Back Cover

This Su-24M Fencer-D of a Russian squadron stationed in Germany was shown at the ILA'92 exposition in Berlin in June, 1992. (Piotr Butowski)

INTRODUCTION

This is the second volume of a set of photo-books in which I shall present all types of military aircraft of the East European Countries, particularly the aircraft of the former Soviet Union.

The different strike aircraft show much more variety than the fighters and interceptors. For example, we have a light, subsonic Crao and, on the other hand, a big 275-ton Blackjack with speed equivalent to Ma=2. Their assignments inside the air forces' organization are also different. The Su-25 Frogfoot attack aircraft belong to ground forces (only in peace time, for the sake of convenience, are the air forces responsible for the training and technical maintenance). The fighter-bombers, as well as tactical and medium range bombers, are under the command of the air forces, whereas the go-ahead for use of heavy intercontinental bombers depends on the high command of the armed forces.

This book, although presenting the newest types of aircraft, is a rather historical one. At the end of 1991, the existence of the Soviet Union came to an end. For some time, (probably not very long), a combined armed forces will exist which will no doubt be divided up among the states later on. Nevertheless, the aircraft will remain the same, although the red star will be replaced by the colorful insignia of the new states.

It was not my intention to present a bare set of photos, therefore the captions should be read as a separate story containing the development, application, versions and characteristics of aircraft. My intention was to make this book an aid in the identification of aircraft, therefore I describe the external and internal differences between them. The individual types of aircraft will be presented in historical succession, from the last days of the Tu-16 Badger up to the aircraft which are now being developed (without any certainty that they will be used in the future by the armed forces).

I would like to thank all the institutions and people who helped by providing photos or information for this book. Also, many thanks to all my friends.

Piotr Butowski

Abbreviations

AAM	-	air-to-air missile
ASM	-	air-to-surface missile
AVMF	-	*Aviatsiya Voenno-Morskovo Flota*, Soviet Naval Aviation
ECM	-	electronic contermeasure
ELINT	-	electronic intelligence
FLIR	-	forward-looking infra-red
LLTV	-	low-light television
PVO	-	*Protivo-Vozdushniaya Oborona*, Soviet Air defense
VTOL	-	vertical take-off and landing
VVS	-	*Voenno-Vozdushniye Sily*, Soviet Air Forces

The Tu-16 Badger medium bomber made her maiden flight on 27 April 1952. About 2,000 aircraft of this type, in versions Badger-A, -B and -C, were made before 1959. The remaining models were transformed from the already built aircraft. Actually, some 475 aircraft of this type are in active service. It is appreciated that the VVS of the late USSR have 80 aircraft in the strike version, 10 tankers, 130 reconnaissance and ECM aircraft. A similar number of Tu-16 aircraft belongs to AVMF: 110 missile carriers, 40 tankers and 105 reconnaissance or ECM aircraft. (Tupolev Design Bureau)

The Tu-16 in its first derivative was a classic free-fall bomber with a fuselage weapons bay large enough for one 9-ton FAB-9000 bomb or a combination of smaller size bombs. The photo shows a Tu-16 Badger-A dropping twelve 250-kg bombs.

Some Tu-16 Badger-A bombers have been adapted for another task: the in-flight refuelling of other aircraft. The wing-to-wing method of refuelling is performed this manner: the Tu-16Z tanker extends a long hose from the starboard wing which is caught by the port side wing of another Tu-16.

The Tu-16K-11-16 Badger-G, with two KSR-2 (AS-5 Kelt) stand-off missiles beneath the wings, came into service in 1968. The Tu-16K-11-16 is used in naval aviation mainly for attacks against large warships.

In the Tu-16K-26 (Badger-G mod) version, the old type of KSR-2 stand-off missiles have been replaced by modern KSR-5 (AS-6 Kingfish). This version of aircraft is used by the AVMF as well as by the VVS. The KSR-5 is a 4,000kg anti-radiation missile. The missile can carry a 1,000kg warload at a distance of 400km with speeds equivalent to Ma=3. (Piotr Butowski)

The Tu-16K-26 in a museum in Monino. The RBP-4 (Short Horn) radar antenna is located under the fuselage nose. A small device in the form of an inverted "T" at the aircraft's nose is the antenna of the Ritsa device used for homing KSR-5 missiles (*Ritsa* is the name of a lake in Georgia). (Piotr Butowski)

In some of the Badger-G mod aircraft, the RBP-4 Short Horn radar under the aircraft's nose has been replaced by a bigger unit installed inside the streamlined aerial under the middle part of fuselage. (Swedish Air Force)

The most powerful strike version of Tu-16 is the Tu-16K-10-26 (Badger-C mod). Besides the K-10 (AS-2 Kipper) missile under the fuselage, there are also two KSR-5 (AS-6 Kingfish) missiles under the wings. The aircraft's nose has been redesigned for much bigger Puff Ball radar, with a range more suitable for the new missiles.

This Tu-16R Badger-D is a special ELINT version designed for naval aviation. Apart from a big radar in the nose, there are also several streamlined aerials for electronic equipment installed in a row under the fuselage.

Another variant of the Tu-16K-10-26 has the under-wing pods for the KSR-5 stand-off missiles and free-fall bomb catches under the fuselage.

A Tu-16P Buket (Badger-J) has been erected as a monument by the Priluki Air Regiment in Ukraine. This version is designed for active, high power, electronic jamming, covering the full range, from A to I. This aerial of Buket jamming unit (*buket* for bouquet), from which the aircraft's name originates, is installed inside the aircraft's nose. A long and narrow aerial of Siren jamming unit (*siren* for lilac) is visible under the middle part of the fuselage. (Piotr Butowski)

Another modified variant of the Tu-16P Buket seen during the take-off. One long antenna of the Siren unit under the bomb bay has been replaced by a series of smaller hemispherical aerials.

Cylindrical antenna of the Buket jamming unit installed inside the nose of a Tu-16P. The navigator's cabin is located in the transparent front part of fuselage with the pilot cockpit above and the RBP-4 radar antenna below. At the starboard side there is a fixed AM-23 23mm cannon with 100 cartridges. The cannon is aimed in fighter-like fashion, i.e., by maneuvering the whole aircraft. (Piotr Butowski)

The defensive armament of Tu-16 consists of six or seven 23mm cannons. The photo shows the bottom double cannon stand covering the sectors 95° to each side, 90° downwards and 2° upwards. (Piotr Butowski)

The gunner/radio operator sits between the two transparent streamlined domes at each side of the fuselage. Apart from operating the radio communication equipment, his duty is to control the bottom cannons. The tail gunner controls the tail cannon turret and operates the PRS-1 Argon (Bee Hind) fire control radar with aerial located above the tail cabin. The double cannon tail stand, with 1,000 cartridges, covers the firing sectors 70° to each side, 60° upwards and 40° downwards. (Piotr Butowski)

For almost forty years of its existence, the Tu-16 Badger has been used many times as a flying laboratory for testing new engines in the air. This aircraft, with various engines suspended under the fuselage, is now used by Ramenskoye flight test center. (Piotr Butowski)

The Tu-95 Bear heavy bomber is unique in the world in its combination of four turboprops and swept flying surfaces. About 250 aircraft of this type were made before 1963. Later the production rate was reduced but the manufacturing was never stopped. Exceptional range and endurance are two of the attributes that have kept the Bear in continuous production for over 30 years. The manufacturing life of the Tu-95 Bear is far longer than that of any other warplane ever built. Besides the Tu-95s designed for the VVS, Tu-142 Bear aircraft were also manufactured for the AVMF to be used for maritime surveillance and anti-submarine missions. The photo shows a basic Tu-95 Bear-A free-fall bomber.

In 1991, the strategic aviation capabilities of the USSR consisted of 142 Bear aircraft, including 65 Tu-95K-22 Bear-G transformed from the earlier Tu-95K-20 Bear-C and -D versions. The Bear-G has a Down Beat radar installed in the nose and provisions for two Kh-22 (AS-4 Kitchen) stand-off missiles under the inboard wing sections. The active jamming system had been installed inside the tailcone, replacing the tail gunner stand typical of other versions.

The remaining 77 Bears are cruise missile-carrying Tu-95MS Bear-H's. The cruise missiles developed at the end of the seventies in the USA surprised the Soviet experts. They quickly developed the missiles of their own and in the early eighties, in Kuibyshev, the full-scale production of the Tu-95MS Bear-H (the platform for cruise missiles) was resumed. The first aircraft achieved initial operational capability in 1984. They are equipped with six Kh-55 (AS-15 Kent) cruise missiles installed in the rotating magazine inside the fuselage with an additional two pairs of these missiles carried under the inboard wing sections. (Andrei Grishchenko)

The nose of the Tu-95MS Bear-H aircraft with Short Horn navigation and bombing radar antenna. The in-flight refuelling probe is seen above. (Piotr Butowski)

The instrument panel in the pilot's cockpit of the Tu-95MS Bear-H is surprisingly ample. Note the co-pilot control wheel at the right hand side. (Piotr Butowski)

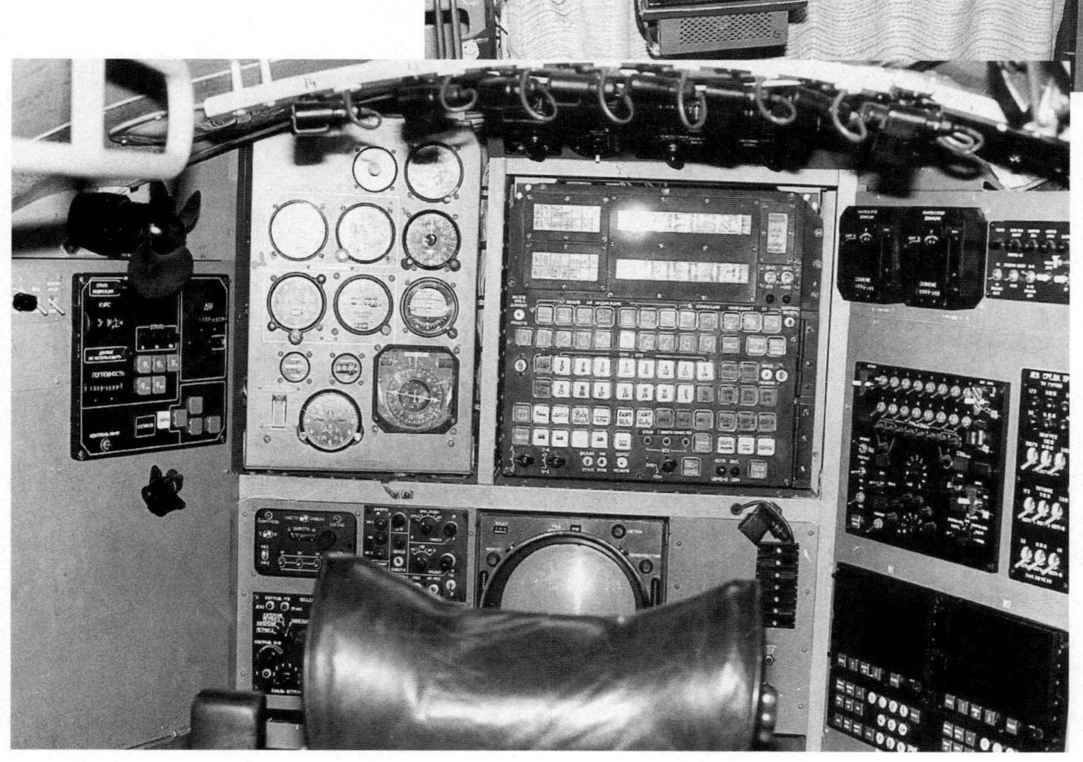

The navigator station is located in the rear part of the hermetic compartment which forms the crew's cabin. The navigator faces the rear of the aircraft. (Piotr Butowski)

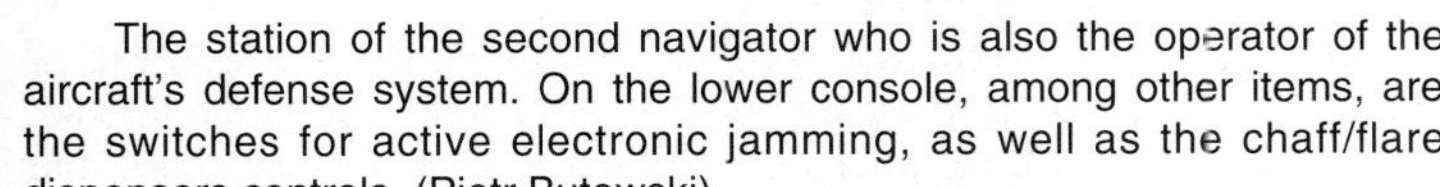

The station of the second navigator who is also the operator of the aircraft's defense system. On the lower console, among other items, are the switches for active electronic jamming, as well as the chaff/flare dispensers controls. (Piotr Butowski)

The station of the communication operator. (Piotr Butowski)

The tail gunner, the seventh crew member of the Tu-95MS, sits in the turret at the rear of fuselage and operates the two twin-barrel GSh-23 cannons. Above the gunner's station is the antenna of the Box Tail warning radar. (Piotr Butowski)

This Tu-95MS, escorted by Su-27s, is being refuelled in flight by an Il-78 Midas flying tanker. (Piotr Butowski)

The Myasishchev M-4 and 3M Bison heavy strategic bombers have never been as widely used as the Tu-95 Bear aircraft. Due to the turbojet engines, Bison aircraft were less economical than Bears. Moreover, the possibilities of their modifications were limited. Because of the design configuration with single-track landing gear, and the engines being located inside the wing roots, Bison could not carry the stand-off missiles. Up to the end of their service in 1987, Bisons were only used as classic bombers. (Piotr Butowski)

Some Bisons have been scrapped. The remaining ones are used as flying tankers for the in-flight refuelling of other long-range aircraft.

This 3MS-2 Bison-B flying tanker is seen in active service (the photos were taken in April 1992). (Piotr Butowski)

A landing 3MS-2 Bison-B with three braking parachutes released from under the fuselage. (Anatoli Andreyev).

The special modified version of the 3M Bison, the VM-T Atlant, was designed for carrying big and heavy loads. Because of turbulence generated by the load carried on the Atlant fuselage, the classic tail section has been replaced by an H-shaped, double tailfin appendage. (Piotr Butowski)

Colonel Pavlyukov and Major Sirotkin brought this example of a 3MD Bison-C to Monino near the Moscow Air Academy airfield in 1986. There it meets its resting place as the 131st flying exhibit of the museum. The 3MD Bison-C, although not as effective and popular as the B-52 or Tu-95, surpasses their looks with its brilliant appearance. (Piotr Butowski)

The tail gunner turret of the 3MD Bison-C aircraft with two AM-23 23mm cannons and, above, the fire control radar antenna. (Piotr Butowski)

Of 1,223 Yak-28 aircraft manufactured between 1960 and 1970, only 50 remain in active service, in two versions: Yak-28PP and Yak-28U. (Piotr Butowski)

A look into the pilot's cockpit of the Yak-28R reconnaissance aircraft. (Piotr Butowski)

Yak-28PP Brewer-E electronic warfare aircraft. A distinguishing feature of this version is the presence of many aerials on the fuselage. (Piotr Butowski)

The crew of Yak-28PP consists of a pilot and a navigator who seats inside the transparent nose of the aircraft. (Piotr Butowski)

A Yak-28R reconnaissance aircraft with the Yak-28U trainer in the background. (Piotr Butowski)

The light attack aircraft Lim-6bis was finally withdrawn from the active service in Polish Air Force in March 1992. Lim-6bis is a Polish-made version of MiG-17 Fresco, used as a light ground attack aircraft. The photo shows the pods under the inboard section of wings (absent in original MiG-17) mounted with UB-16 57mm rocket launchers. (Piotr Butowski)

An Lim-6bis being prepared for flight. Note the lowered cannon mount under the aircraft nose with one 37mm and two 23mm cannons. (Piotr Butowski)

The SBlim-2A is a reconnaissance version of the MiG-15UTI two-seater, with cameras located under the fuselage. This version is used by Polish naval aviation. (Piotr Butowski)

The Tu-22 Blinder was designed as a supersonic successor of the Tu-16 Badger. However, the replacement was not an easy task. The only advantage of the Tu-22 in respect to the Tu-16 is the greater speed at high altitudes. On the other hand, the range of the Tu-22 is shorter and the operation more difficult. Therefore, only about 250 Tu-22 aircraft were made, much less than the number of Tu-16s manufactured. (Anatoli Andreyev)

The first Tu-22 Blinder aircraft entered active service in the mid-1960s. The actual number used by the former USSR was 175 (150 in VVS and 25 in AVMF). (Boris Vdovenko)

The outstanding feature of the Tu-22 Blinder is the position of its engines which are installed side-by-side on the rear part of the fuselage near the root of the tail fin. This gives the aircraft unique silhouette. Note the movable, single-barrel cannon in the aircraft tail. The cannon is automatically controlled by means of radar, the antenna being installed under the engine nozzles. (Piotr Butowski)

The first Tu-22 Blinder-A aircraft were basic bombers with a fuselage weapons bay suitable for free-fall nuclear and conventional bombs. There was no in-flight refuelling probe on nose. (Piotr Butowski)

The Tu-22K Blinder-B missile carrier is equipped with larger radar and an in-flight refuelling probe on nose. The weapons bay was redesigned to carry one Kh-22 (AS-4 Kitchen) stand-off missile, semi-recessed under fuselage.

A pair of Tu-22K Blinder-B medium range missile carrier. (Piotr Butowski)

The Tu-22 Blinder-C reconnaissance version has a slimmer nose and six camera windows in the weapons bay doors. (Swedish Air Force)

A Tu-22 Blinder landing with braking parachutes open.

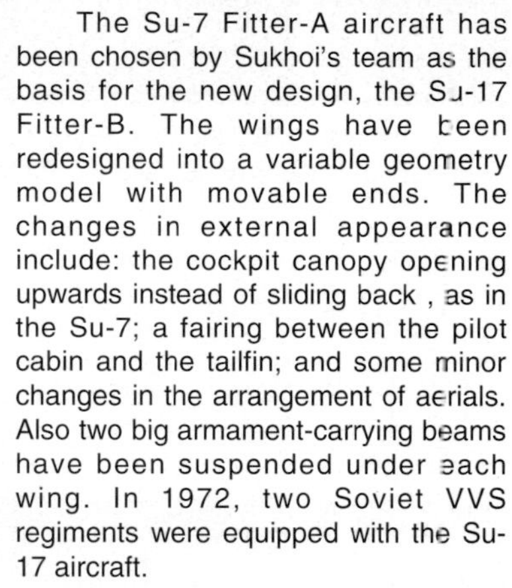

The Su-7 Fitter-A aircraft has been chosen by Sukhoi's team as the basis for the new design, the Su-17 Fitter-B. The wings have been redesigned into a variable geometry model with movable ends. The changes in external appearance include: the cockpit canopy opening upwards instead of sliding back , as in the Su-7; a fairing between the pilot cabin and the tailfin; and some minor changes in the arrangement of aerials. Also two big armament-carrying beams have been suspended under each wing. In 1972, two Soviet VVS regiments were equipped with the Su-17 aircraft.

In 1972, the new variant Su-17M Fitter-C replaced the Su-17 on the production line in Komsomolsk on Amur. The most important innovation was the Lyulka AL-21F3 engine, a whole generation ahead of the former AL-7F-1. The export designation of Su-17M model is Su-20. (Piotr Butowski)

In the late 1970s, the Su-17M (Su-20) aircraft was adapted for carrying KKR-1 reconnaissance containers. (Piotr Butowski)

The KKR-1 container is 6.9m long and contains three cameras, a Virazh ELINT unit and illuminating flares. (Piotr Butowski)

The Su-20 Fitter-C belonging to 7th Bomber-Reconnaissance Air Regiment in Powidz, Poland, being prepared for flight. (Piotr Butowski)

A look into the cockpit of a Su-17M (Su-20) Fitter-C. (Piotr Butowski)

The B–8 is actually the most popular rocket laurcher is the air forces of the late Warsaw Pact. It can carry twenty S-8 80mm rockets. (Piotr Butowski)

A Su-20R Fitter-C during the engine test prior to take-off on a reconnaissance flight. The thin line entering the air intake is a puddle, left after recent rain, being sucked out. (Piotr Butowski)

In 1976, the serial manufacturing of the Su-17M2 Fitter-D (the export name being "Su-22") began. The external appearance of the Su-17M2 was similar to the Su-17M except for the nose of fuselage, which has been extended by 40cm. This nose contained the most important improvements - a Fon (*fon* for background) laser rangefinder installed inside the air intake cone. Also, a large wide tub containing the DISS-7 Doppler navigation radar appeared under the nose of the Su-17M2.

A Soviet Su-17M2 Fitter-D with a UB-32 rocket launcher and auxiliary fuel tank suspended beneath the wing. Note the opened airbrakes at the rear of the fuselage.

The design of the Su-17 fuselage was changed considerably in 1977. From the Su-17M3 Fitter-H version on, the fuselage was lowered due to the absence of the bottom dome of the Doppler navigation radar, which was present on the Su-17M2 Fitter-D. On the other hand, a hump housing avionics equipment appeared behind the pilot cockpit canopy. The tailfin was increased in order to compensate for the larger front section.

The Su-17M3 Fitter-H is armed with Kh-23 (AS-7 Kerry) radio-command guided air-to-surface missiles, R-13M (AA-2 Atoll) infra-red homing air-to-air missiles, as well as UB-32 rocket pods. (Sukhoi Design Bureau)

A Su-17M3 aircraft with the factory number of 22301 in Monino museum. Production of the Su-17 came to an end in 1990. There are 755 aircraft of this type still in active service in the air forces of the former USSR. Several hundred others are used by a dozen or so countries throughout the world. (Piotr Butowski)

The Su-17UM3 Fitter-G is a two-seater, training version of Su-17M3. The photo shows this aircraft in Polish colors, bearing the export designation of Su-22UM3K. (Piotr Butowski)

The standard propulsion system of the Su-17 aircraft is the Lyulka AL-21F3 engine. However, some aircraft are equipped with the Tumanski R-29BS-300 engine. The Su-17 with the R-29 was made mainly for export; only a small number of them can be found in the USSR. Fortunately for aircraft lovers and spies, the diameter of the R-29 engine is significantly larger than the AL-21, therefore the fuselage of the Su-17 with the R-29 engine is thicker at its rear, allowing easy identification of these two variants. The photo shows a Su-17UMK Fitter-E with the R-29BS-300 engine. (Piotr Butowski)

The most conspicuous external feature of Su-17M4 Fitter-K, when compared with the earlier versions, is a small air intake for air cooling the avionics, located at the tailfin root. The aircraft is equipped with the newest navigational-aiming system, the PrNK-54 with a digital board computer. (Piotr Butowski)

During the building of the Su-17M4, a critical review of the aircraft design was made and some changes were introduced. Thanks to the replacement of the movable air intake cone with a fixed one, the aircraft's weight has been reduced and its speed limited to Ma=1.8. The old type Fon laser unit in the nose cone has been replaced by the modern Klon device (*klon* for mapletree), which is not only a range finder but also a target designator. (Piotr Butowski)

A Czecho-Slovakian Su-22M4K Fitter-K in inverted flight. (Piotr Butowski)

The final Fitter product, the Su-17M4 Fitter-K, manufactured serially in 1980-1990, was named the Su-22M4K for export. The photo shows a Polish Su-22M4K. The Polish Air Force uses 86 aircraft of this version and also 19 Su-22UM3K two-seaters. (Piotr Butowski)

The pilot's cockpit in "humpback" versions of the Su-17 (the cockpit of Su-22M4K is in the picture) is much wider and more comfortable than in previous versions. (Piotr Butowski)

The new cockpit was equipped with the new K-36DM ejection seat, which is still standard equipment for all the contemporary Soviet aircraft. (Piotr Butowski)

For many years, the necessity of jamming devices was underestimated by the Soviets. They learned their lesson during Afghanistan War. After 1980, the Fitters were equipped with more and more devices called "Afghan tricks" by Soviet pilots. In the extreme case, they included four KDS-23 chaff/flare dispensers built into the hump behind the cockpit, eight ASO-2 cassettes with 32 charges each at the back of fuselage, and four more ASO-2s, under the fuselage. Left photo shows ASO-2 dispensers installed on the fuselage of a Su-22M4K (note also the small air intake at the tailfin root). Right photo shows the same dispensers at the bottom of fuselage. (Piotr Butowski)

The board computer introduced into the Su-17M4 Fitter-K aircraft made it possible to bring to life the old idea of Soviet designers - the directional cannons of a fighter plane. The Su-17M4 can carry SPPU-22-01 cannon containers. In the front section of the container there is one GSh-23 twin-barrel cannon. The barrels are installed on movable mounts, which can be lowered by 23°. The munitions and controls are located in the rear section of the container. The SPPU container can be mounted with the muzzles directed forward or backward. The cannons, after being initially aimed by the pilot, are then controlled by the computer. (Piotr Butowski)

The fully-armed Fitter-K with SPPU-22-01 gun containers, R-60 (AA-8 Aphid) AAM (for self-defence) and a B-8 rocket launcher. Note the SPPU container suspended under the fuselage as well as the six-tube KDS-23 chaff/flare dispensers built onto the back of fuselage. (Piotr Butowski)

Shown here are 50kg bombs on the MBD-3 multiple weapons rack beneath the wing of Fitter-K. (Piotr Butowski)

The heaviest of all Russian unguided rockets is the over-calibre S-25 in two variants: S-25OF in a single-use O-25 launcher and the modified S-25OFM with a fragmentation warhead (foreground). (Piotr Butowski)

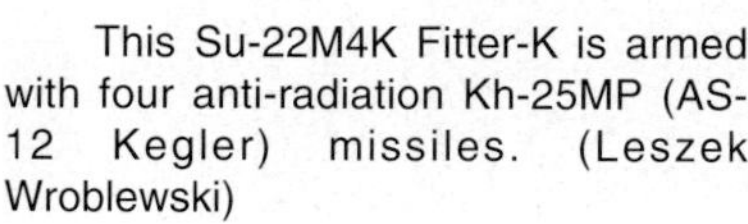

This Su-22M4K Fitter-K is armed with four anti-radiation Kh-25MP (AS-12 Kegler) missiles. (Leszek Wroblewski)

There are three versions of Kh-25 module air-to-surface missile: anti-radiation Kh-25MP (AS-12 Kegler), laser guided Kh-25ML (AS-10 Karen), as well as radio-command guided Kh-25MR (AS-10 Karen). The Kh-25 missile is a standard armament of former Soviet strike aircraft. (Piotr Butowski)

FAB-500M-62 (model 1962), a standard Russian demolition bomb (in the foreground), BetAB-500ShP bomb designed to destroy concrete fortifications and runways (next in line) as well as FAB-500ShN bomb (third in the row). (Piotr Butowski)

Russian cluster bombs: RBK-500AO-2.5RT cassette containing 108 AO-2.5RT bomblets (foreground), with RBK-500ShOAB-0.5 containing 565 bomblets behind it. (Piotr Butowski)

The Russian heavy guided bombs. KAB-500KR TV-guided bomb in the foreground, and KAB-500L laser-guided bomb behind it. (Piotr Butowski)

The MiG-23 Flogger was designed as a multi purpose aircraft, therefore the fighter variant was soon followed by the fighter-bomber MiG-23B Flogger-F. The airframe remained unchanged except the front part, from which the radar has been removed. The beveled bottom of the aircraft nose and increased cockpit windows improve the ground visibility. The aircraft with the side number "321" is the first prototype of the MiG-23B Flogger-F fighter-bomber tested in flight on 20 August 1970. The aircraft designation in the Mikoyan Design Bureau was "Product 32", like the side number. A total number of twenty-four aircraft of this version (equipped with Lyulka AL-21F-3 engines) were made. (Piotr Butowski)

The weapons system of the MiG-23B has been thoroughly changed compared to the MiG-23. The RP-23 air intercept radar has been removed and the DISS-7 Doppler navigational radar, the ASP-17 gunsight and the PBK-3 bombsight have been installed. The wing of the MiG-23B did not yet have the leading edge dent, which is the characteristic feature of all later versions of the MiG-23 and MiG-27. There is no laser rangefinder opening on the aircraft's nose as they are on all later attack versions. (Piotr Butowski)

The modified version of the MiG-23BN came into being soon after the MiG-23B. The new version was propelled by the Tumanski R-29B-300 engine and was equipped with the new navigational-aiming system Sokol-23N (*sokol* for falcon) with the Fon laser rangefinder. Cockpit armor has been added, including external side plates. The photo shows a Czecho-Slovakian MiG-23BN Flogger-F aircraft. (Vaclav Jukl)

This view of the MiG-27 clearly shows problems which had to be overcome by the designers in order to obtain sufficient wheel traction for the landing gear. The opening for the Fon laser rangefinder can be seen on the aircraft nose. Below, protruding from both sides, are the aerials of radar warning receivers. The Delta unit antenna and the camera gun are seen on the fixed parts of wings. (Piotr Butowski)

More serious modifications have been introduced into the design of the MiG-27 Flogger-D fighter-bomber version in order to improve the aircraft's ability to attacking ground targets. Assuming that great speed is not necessary for a fighter-bomber, the designers replaced the adjustable air intakes with fixed ones. The MiG-27 can be easily distinguished from the MiG-23B by the absence of the adjusting plates in front of the engine air intakes. The airframe structure was reinforced so that the MiG-27 could carry 4,000kg of bombs instead of 3,000kgs like the MiG-23B. (Piotr Butowski)

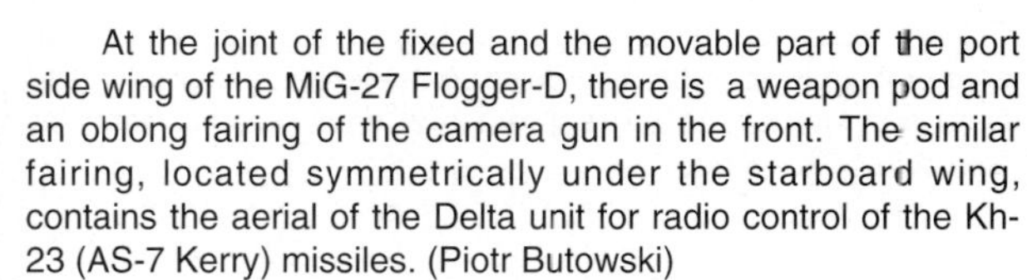

At the joint of the fixed and the movable part of the port side wing of the MiG-27 Flogger-D, there is a weapon pod and an oblong fairing of the camera gun in the front. The similar fairing, located symmetrically under the starboard wing, contains the aerial of the Delta unit for radio control of the Kh-23 (AS-7 Kerry) missiles. (Piotr Butowski)

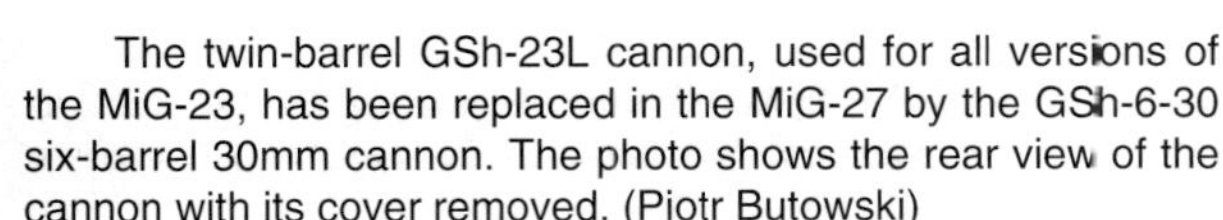

The twin-barrel GSh-23L cannon, used for all versions of the MiG-23, has been replaced in the MiG-27 by the GSh-6-30 six-barrel 30mm cannon. The photo shows the rear view of the cannon with its cover removed. (Piotr Butowski)

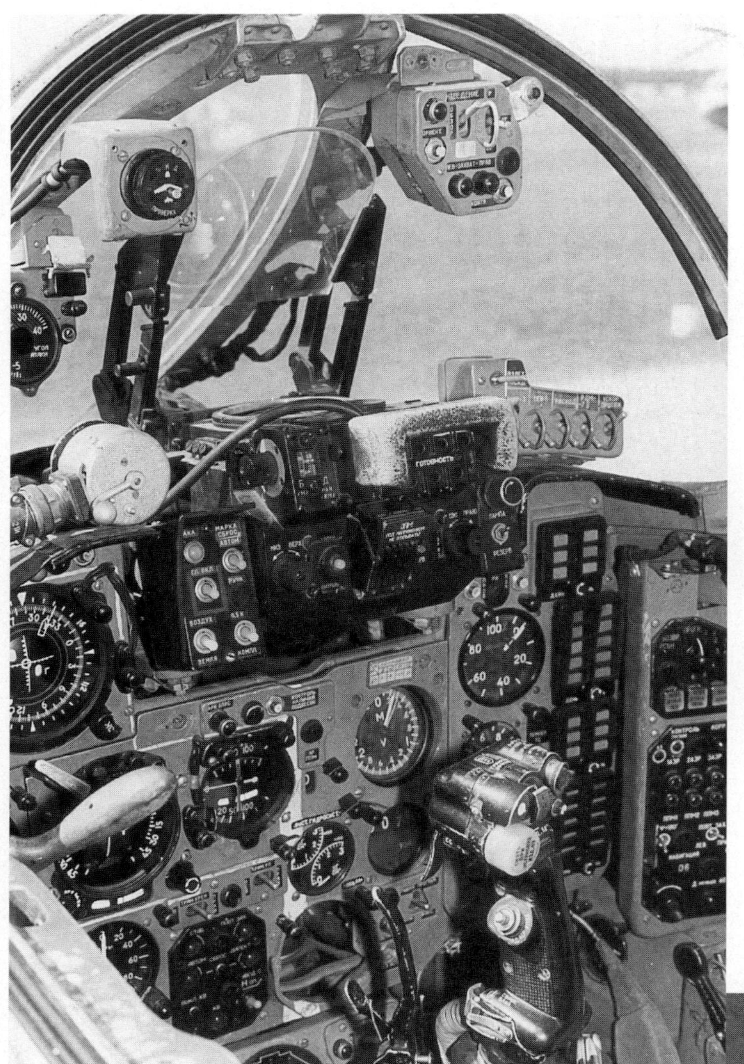

The cockpit of the MiG-27 Flogger-D is rather small, particularly when compared to its competitor, the Sukhoi Su-22 Fitter. (Piotr Butowski)

The wide, low-pressure tires of the MiG-27 main wheels allow the aircraft to be operated from unpaved airfields. A catch for the 100kg bomb is visible near the landing gear. (Piotr Butowski)

The most outstanding features of the MiG-27M Flogger-J version are long leading edge wing root extensions. Also, the configuration of aerials on the aircraft nose has been changed. The Fon laser rangefinder Fon has been replaced by the Klon laser unit, which can be also used as the target designator. The Delta unit aerial and the camera gun disappeared from the fixed part of the wing.

A MIG-27M Flogger-J aircraft during an exercise in removing radioactive contamination. Note that the servicemen wear protective rubber cloaks.

The newest modification of the MiG-27 is the MiG-27K Flogger-J with the new Kaira TV-controlled weapon system. (Piotr Butowski)

The streamlined antenna of the radio-control missile system on the upper part of MiG-27K Flogger-J nose. Below the nose is the LLTV camera and the laser rangefinder/target designator window. (Piotr Butowski)

The nose of the MiG-27 aircraft with the additional armor plate clearly seen on the side of the cockpit. (Piotr Butowski)

The T-6-1 is the first prototype of the Su-24 tactical bomber. With a delta-shaped wing of small surface area, the aircraft is externally similar to the British TSR.2. The T-6-1 was tested in flight in June 1967. Four additional lift engines are arranged vertically in the middle section of fuselage. (Sukhoi Design Bureau)

ASO-2 chaff/flare dispensers installed on the back of the MiG-27 fuselage. (Piotr Butowski)

A T-6-1 aircraft displayed at the Monino museum near Moscow. During tests, the cockpit canopy was torn apart and cut off the top of the tailfin (note the tailfin is shorter than on other Su-24 aircraft). The T-6-1 was later used as a flying stand for testing the equipment and weapons. (Piotr Butowski)

T-6-2 prototype with variable geometry wings came into being in 1970. (Sukhoi Design Bureau)

A pair of fully-armed Tu-16K-26 Badger-G mod missile carriers. (Piotr Butowski)

The nose of the Tu-95MS Bear-H aircraft with Short Horn navigation and bombing radar antenna. The in-flight refuelling probe is seen above. (Piotr Butowski)

This Tu-95MS, escorted by Su-27s, is being refuelled in flight by an Il-78 Midas flying tanker. (Piotr Butowski)

Myasishchev 3MS-2 tanker in service with the Russian strategic aviation regiment based at Engels, near Saratov on Volga. (Anatoli Andreyev)

The 3M Bison (special modified version), formerly called the 3M-T and later the VM-T Atlant, was designed for carrying big and heavy loads (particularly parts of the Energia rocket and the Buran space-shuttle). (Piotr Butowski)

Yak-28PP. The UB-16-57 launcher under the outer wing houses sixteen S-5P chaff/flare rockets. (Piotr Butowski)

The Lim-6bis is a Polish-made version of the MiG-17 Fresco, used as a light ground attack aircraft. (Piotr Butowski)

The Tu-22U Blinder-D is a training version with a raised cockpit for the instructor aft of the standard flight deck, and a step-up canopy. (Anatoli Andreyev)

A Tu-22KD Blinder-B getting ready for the take-off. (Anatoli Andreyev)

The airfield of the Polish 7th Bomber-Reconnaissance Air Regiment. A Su-20R Fitter-C is seen in the foreground with a Su-22UM3K Fitter-G in the background. (Piotr Butowski)

MiG-27K Flogger-J. The production of the MiG-27 aircraft came to an end in 1984. There are 805 aircraft of this type in active service in the former USSR. (Piotr Butowski)

A Su-24M is refuelled in air by another of the same aircraft using the UPAZ universal refuelling device.

Note not only the different camouflage scheme of this Su-24M but also the opened aerodynamic brakes in front of the landing gear under the fuselage. There are also chaff/flare dispensers installed in the aerodynamic fences on the upper surface of wings. (Piotr Butowski)

MiG–27K armed with a Kh–31P anti–radiation missile. (Protr Butowski)

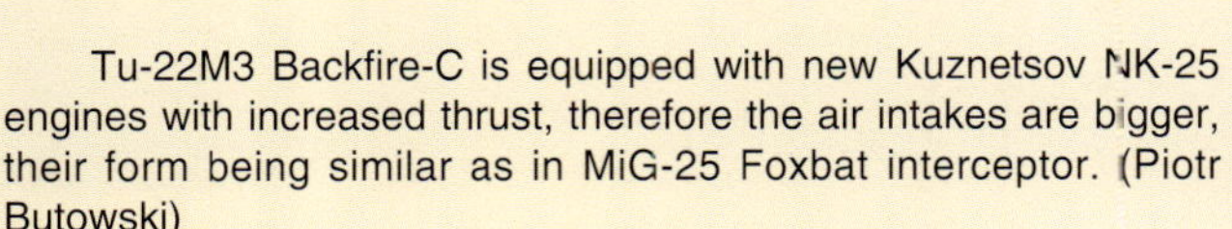

Tu-22M3 Backfire-C is equipped with new Kuznetsov NK-25 engines with increased thrust, therefore the air intakes are bigger, their form being similar as in MiG-25 Foxbat interceptor. (Piotr Butowski)

Tu-22M3 Backfire-C when taking-off. (Piotr Butowski)

Two Tu-22M3 Backfire-C bombers. Note the different versions of Kh-22 (AS-4 Kitchen) stand-off missiles carried by both aircraft. The first one carries the anti-radar version, while the second one is equipped with missiles with programmable trajectory and an integral navigation system. (Piotr Butowski)

A twin-barrel 30mm cannon dismounted from the fuselage of a Su-25. (Piotr Butowski)

Unlike the combat version, the Su-25UB Frogfoot-B has a two-seat cockpit. The rear seat is raised considerably, giving a humpbacked appearance. A separate hinged portion of the framed canopy is over each cockpit. Also, the tailfin is significantly taller.

A Su-25UB in low-level flight. (Piotr Butowski)

A Su-25 from the 60th Attack Air Regiment in Sital-chai (Azerbaijan), the first unit armed with Su-25s since 1981. (Piotr Butowski)

Su-25T aircraft shown during the exposition for CIS leaders in Minsk, February 1992. (Dmitri Grinyuk)

Aircraft with the side number "31" taxiing before take-off. Unlike the remaining machines, she has the old type relief-suction doors with five slots at the air intake sides; other aircraft have six slots. (Piotr Butowski)

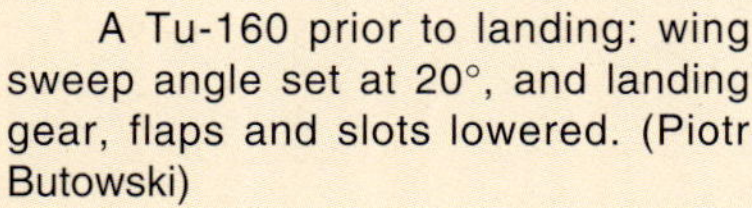

A Tu-160 prior to landing: wing sweep angle set at 20°, and landing gear, flaps and slots lowered. (Piotr Butowski)

The serial production began in 1972 in Novosybirsk factory under the designation of Su-24 Fencer-A. The first regiment equipped with these aircraft became operational in December 1972. Yak-28 Brewer front-line bombers were gradually replaced by Su-24. The photo shows a Su-24 with the factory number 0515304, meaning it is the fourth aircraft of fifth production series made in Novosybirsk Factory No.153. (Piotr Butowski)

One of the first Su-24 aircraft produced. The air intakes are much larger than in the later aircraft. Also the tip of nose is different. The most interesting, although not very well visible detail is the SPPU-6 gun container suspended from the underwing pylon, which holds a six-barrel GSh-6-23 23mm movable cannon. The computer-controlled cannon can be lowered by about 30°. The photo shows the barrels in the lowered position. (Sukhoi Design Bureau)

Manufacture of the Su-24 Fencer has continued since 1972, though the production rate is now much lower. In the very near future, production will probably come to an end in favor of the strike version of the Su-27 Flanker. There are 1,085 Su-24 still in active service in the aviation of the former USSR; those include 840 bombers and 235 reconnaissance and ECM aircraft in the VVS and 10 reconnaissance Su-24s used by the AVMF. The photo shows the Su-24M Fencer-D. (Piotr Butowski)

This view shows the rectangular shape of the rear of fuselage as well as the small container for the braking parachute at the root of tailfin. The antenna installed on the tailfin just below the rudder belongs to the Sirena radar warning receiver (*sirena* for siren). These are typical features of the Su-24 Fencer-A. This aircraft was manufactured up to the 15th production series. (Swedish Air Force)

The Western name for the successor Su-24 aircraft was Fencer-B, though in the USSR the new suffix was not used. The new NATO code resulted from some changes which, although insignificant in regards to combat ability, made the aircraft externally distinctive. For example, the housing for the braking parachute was increased in size and raised up, and the fuselage end near the engine outlet nozzle was rounded up. The photo shows a Fencer-B aircraft with underwing fuel tanks which hold 3,000 liters each.

The rear section of the fuselage, with its large braking-parachute housing is typical of all versions of the Su-24, except the Fencer-A. (Piotr Butowski)

A Su-24 Fencer-B with Kh-29L (AS-14 Kedge) laser-guided ASMs suspended under the fuselage and under fixed sections of wings. Kh-25ML (AS-10 Karen) missiles are carried under the movable sections of wings. Note that this version has the large aerodynamic fence on the wing which is uncommon in this model. (Sukhoi Design Bureau)

The Fencer-C (called simply the Su-24 in the former USSR) is equipped with different warning equipment from that of the Fencer-B. Big aerials are installed on the tailfin as well as at the upper part of the air intakes. From this version on, the air intakes became non-adjustable in order to reduce the structural weight by 236kg.

The Su-24M Fencer-D entered the production line in Novosybirsk and active service in the VVS in 1978. A new weapons system was developed for this version. Also, the accuracy and reliability of the navigational-aiming system has been improved. A part of the radioelectronic equipment was replaced by a new system too. Note the Kh-29L (AS-14 Kedge) laser-guided ASM under the fixed section of wing, and the bombs suspended under the movable wing panels and under the fuselage. (Sukhoi Design Bureau)

There are two versions of the heavy Kh-29 (AS-14 Kedge) air-to-air surface missile: laser guided Kh-29L (in the foreground) and TV Kh-29T. Kh-29 is designed mainly for destroying armored targets. (Piotr Butowski)

Th is clearly visible that the nose of the Su-24 Fencer-D is longer when compared with former versions. The pylons installed on the fixed sections of wings are enlarged and connected with the aerodynamic fences. More classical and straight, with winglets indicating the angles of attack and glide, is the nose probe, which in the former versions was made in the form of sophisticated, three-story structure. (Sukhoi Design Bureau)

A Su-24M with two additional 3,000 liter fuel tanks under the wings. Note the way of opening the cockpit canopy, with two separate hatches above each seat. (Sukhoi Design Bureau)

The Su-24M is equipped with an in-flight refuelling system in order to increase its flying range and the payload. The aircraft, which is stationed on the dirt airfield, can take-off with full payload, without fuel reserve, and is then refueled in the air. The protruding fuel receptacle is seen in the front of this Su-24M Fencer-D. (Dmitri Grinyuk)

The in-flight refuelling probe of the Su-24M. (Dmitri Grinyuk)

In the summer of 1985, the air force of the Baltic Fleet obtained a squadron of Su-24MR Fencer-E bomber-reconnaissance aircraft. This aircraft carried no weapons except defensive air-to-air missiles. The cannon was replaced by cameras. This Su-24MR, photographed over the Baltic Sea, carries the reconnaissance containers: Shtil-2M under the fuselage and Efir-1M under the movable section of starboard wing. The fuel tanks are suspended under the fixed sections of the wings. (Swedish Air Force)

The Su-24 Fencer had been paid many compliments in the West: "The most lethal warplane in the Soviet inventory", "technologically the most advanced aircraft". Su-24 Fencer can carry 8,000kg of weapons, flying at 1,400km/h at sea level with automatic terrain avoidance. This tactical radius of action at low altitudes exceeds 500km. (Piotr Butowski)

A Kh-58 (AS-11 Kilter) anti-radiation missile under the Su-24MK Fencer-D. (Piotr Butowski)

The Su-24 was the first Soviet aircraft to have an adjustable pylon at the movable section of wing; the pylon is always parallel to the aircraft axis. In this photo the pylon carries MBD-3 multiple weapons racks with six 50kg bombs. (Piotr Butowski)

This paint scheme of the Su-24M (with colored upper side of the aircraft) is not a typical one. The small, hemispherical dome at the back of fuselage contains the satellite navigation aerial. (Piotr Butowski)

Double bomb racks under the fixed section of wing. It can carry two 500kg bombs or two B-8 rocket launchers. (Piotr Butowski)

A view of the underside of a Su-24M Fencer-D. The big window of the Kaira-24 LLTV device is seen in the middle section with the bomb-carrying beams behind. There are two identical oblong fairings on both sides. The port-side fairing, with the black mark in the photo, contains a six-barrel Gsh-6-23 cannon. The barrel shutters are opened before firing. The contents of the starboard-side fairing is unknown. (Piotr Butowski)

The crew of the Su-24 includes two persons: a pilot and a navigator/weapons system operator. Their K-36D ejection seats are arranged side-by-side in a rather small cockpit. The fuselage is about 1.5m wide. There is plenty of equipment in the cockpit. In the foreground you can see a big, rubber radar eyepiece. (Piotr Butowski)

The export variant of the Su-24M is called the Su-24MK (K stands for *Kommercheski,* or commercial). The photo shows an Su-24MK on display at Khodinka airfield in Moscow in August, 1989. (Piotr Butowski)

A Su-24M Fencer D landing with opened braking parachutes. (Pictr Butowski)

A Su-24M Fencer-D when landing. (Piotr Butowski)

A Su-24M Fencer D at Kubinka airfield near Moscow. (Piotr Butowski)

The light attack aircraft developed jointly by Rumania and the former Yugoslavia bears two different names: Orao in Yugoslavia and IAR-93 in Rumania. Production of the series has continued from 1979 in both Rumania and Yugoslavia. The photos show two Yugoslavian Oraos.

Rumanian IAR-93 with a garland of twelve 100kg bombs.

The Tu-22M Backfire is a successor to the Tu-16 Badger and Tu-22 Blinder. This aircraft entered active service in the mid-seventies. Like its predecessors, this is an intermediate range bomber carrying up to 9,000kg of armament. Its speed amounts to Ma=2 and its range is equal to 5,500km. There are 195 Backfires now in the VVS and 125 in the AVMF of the former USSR. The photos show two Tu-22M2 Backfire-B aircraft flying with fully swept outer wing panels during exercises in East Germany in 1980. (Ireneusz Sobieszczuk)

This very rare photo of very poor quality shows the Tu-22M Backfire-A in active service. Only twenty aircraft of this model were built. Unlike the more numerous later versions, the Backfire-A has large elliptic fairings on the wings. (Alexei Matryonin)

The Tu-22M Backfire-A with factory number 5019029 is on display at the Monino museum. (Piotr Butowski)

A look under the nose of the Tu-22M Backfire-A. The inflight refuelling probe can be seen above the front radar. The crew consists of four airmen. Two pilots sit in the front part of the cabin, the rear seats are occupied by the navigator and the weapons system officer. The cover of the TV-camera assisting the navigator/weapons system officer is seen at the left hand side in the lower part. (Piotr Butowski)

This Tu-22M2 Backfire-B is an early variation of this model. Note the elliptical Box Tail warning-radar housing and two twin-barrel GSh-23 cannons under it. The long in-flight refuelling probe can be seen on the nose. (Swedish Air Force)

The Tu-22M Backfire was an object of much controversy during the SALT-2 talks. The aircraft was to be considered a non-strategic weapon provided that they would not be stationed in Arctic regions, that the production rate would be limited to thirty aircraft per year, and that the aircraft would not be equipped with missiles with a range exceeding 600km. Also, the ability to be refuelled in the air had to be limited. Therefore, the refuelling equipment was removed from the Tu-22M2 Backfire-B. This aircraft also has the new form of Box Tail radome. (Swedish Air Force)

The Tu-22M3 Backfire-C is equipped with new Kuznetsov NK-25 engines which provide increased thrust, therefore the air intakes are bigger; their form is similar to those on the MiG-25 Foxbat interceptor. (Piotr Butowski)

The tail of a Tu-22M3 Backfire-C, with only one GSh-23 cannon instead of two cannons in the former version. (Piotr Butowski)

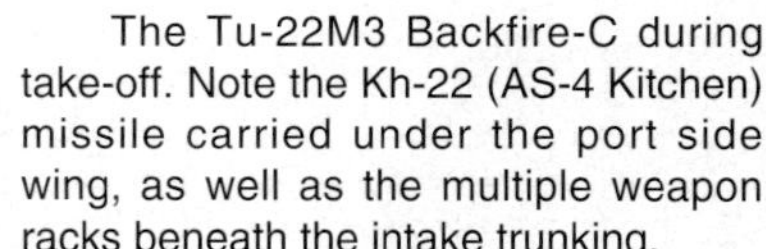

The Tu-22M3 Backfire-C during take-off. Note the Kh-22 (AS-4 Kitchen) missile carried under the port side wing, as well as the multiple weapon racks beneath the intake trunking.

A Tu-22M3 Backfire-C with wings fully extended, opened slots, lowered flaps and landing gear. The bomb bay (seen in the middle section) was designed for Kh-22 missiles, though there are also missile carrying pylons installed under the fixed sections of the wings.

Two Tu-22M3 Backfire-C bombers. Note the different versions of Kh-22 (AS-4 Kitchen) stand-off missiles carried by both aircraft. The first one carries the anti-radar version, while the second one is equipped with missiles with programmable trajectory and an integral navigation system. (Piotr Butowski)

The Kh-22 (AS-4 Kitchen) rocket-powered missile under the wing of a Tu-22M3.

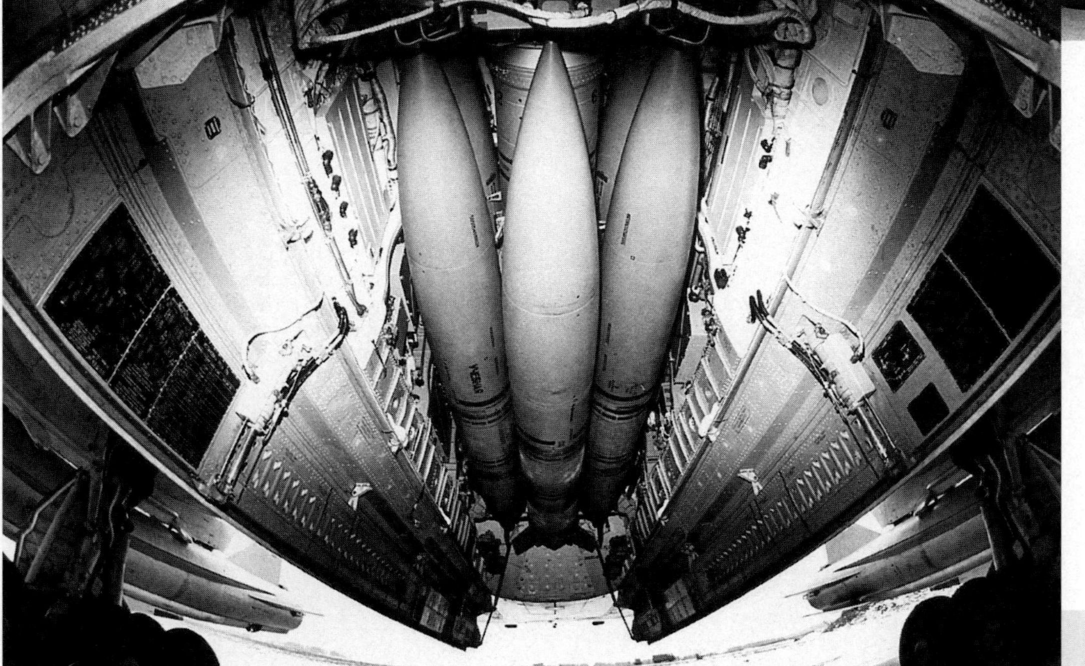

The Kh-15P (AS-16 Kickback) anti-radar missiles can be carried on a rotary launcher inside the fuselage of the Tu-22M3. These weapons are used to destroy opposing air defense radar sites.

A Tu-22M3 Backfire-C from Poltava heavy bomber regiment, one of the five Backfire regiments based in Ukraine. (Piotr Butowski)

The Su-25 Frogfoot is the first Soviet close-support attack aircraft to be developed after many years. This is a subsonic machine with strong armor and a powerful weapons system. It entered active service in 1980, when first aircraft of this type went to Afghanistan. There are 330 aircraft of this type now in service in the former USSR, one hundred other machines have been exported. The Su-25 is manufactured in Tbilisi factory in Georgia. (Sukhoi Design Bureau)

Su-25 Frogfoots at the Sital-chai air base in Azerbaijan. In the foreground you can see the spike laid on the runway as a security measure against possible abduction (this is the frontier zone). (Piotr Butowski)

The Su-25 Frogfoot-A can carry up to 4,000kg of weapons on eight underwing pods. The last two small pylons are used for R-60 (AA-8 Aphid) AAMs. (Piotr Butowski)

A Su-25 Frogfoot-A armed with eight B-8 rocket launchers and two R-60 close air combat AAMs for self defense. (Piotr Butowski)

The low-pressure main landing gear tire of the Su-25, with a glimpse of a dismantled wing above. The wing structure is a double-spar type with ample torque box between the spars. (Piotr Butowski)

The split rudder of the Su-25 Frogfoot. The small upper rudder section is operated through sensor vanes and transducers on the nose probe, and the automatic electro-mechanical yaw-dumping system. A small air intake for cooling the electronic equipment and cockpit ventilation is seen in the lowest part of the tailfin's leading edge. (Piotr Butowski)

The Klon laser rangefinder and target designator's window in the nose of the Su-25 Frogfoot A. Note the twin-barrel 30mm cannon on the bottom of the front fuselage, on the port side. (Piotr Butowski)

The cockpit of the Su-25BM Frogfoot-A. (Piotr Butowski)

This vertical plate on the wing-tip fairing is not an aerial. It has been installed to obscure the landing floodlights and to protect the pilot's eyes from being blinded. (Piotr Butowski)

The export version of the Su-25, like this aircraft of the Czecho-Slovakian Air Force, is designated with the additional suffix "K" kommercheski, or commercial. (Piotr Butowski)

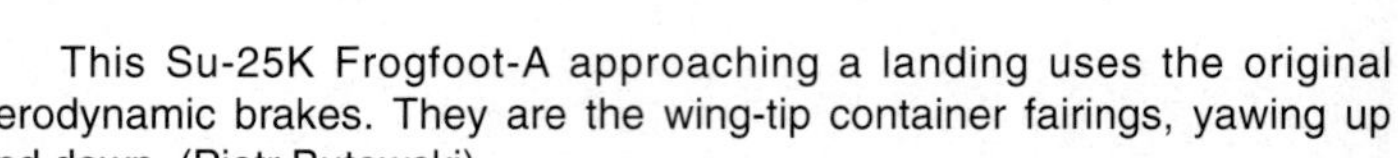

This Su-25K Frogfoot-A approaching a landing uses the original aerodynamic brakes. They are the wing-tip container fairings, yawing up and down. (Piotr Butowski)

Close-up view of the aerodynamic brakes. As can be seen, they are not simply split flaps. They are opened in two stages, with a small flap opening forward of the main flap. (Sukhoi Design Bureau)

The Su-25BM is equipped with the new R-195 engines with the thrust increased up to 44.1 kN (4,500kG). The Su-25BM can be easily differentiated from the Su-25 by the cylinder protruding from the center of the exhaust nozzle. An additional cooling air intake appeared on the engine nacelle. There are also two ASO-2, 32-tube chaff/flare dispensers. (Piotr Butowski)

The Su-25 Frogfoot is powered by two Tumanski R-95Sh engines, of 40.2kN (4,100kG) of thrust each, which are non-afterburner versions of the MiG-21's engines. (Piotr Butowski)

Four ASO-2 cassettes are installed inside the long end of fuselage of the Su-25. At the very end is the opened cover of the braking parachute hatch. (Piotr Butowski)

The tandem two-seat Su-25UB Frogfoot-B came into being in 1985. This version is used for training the pilots of attack aircraft. (Piotr Butowski)

A Su-25UB. Note the auxiliary fuel tank under the aircraft wings. (Piotr Butowski)

A Su-25 Frogfoot-A at the Kubinka airfield near Moscow. (Piotr Butowski)

In 1992, the manufacture of the Su-25T begins. Inside the Sukhoi design bureau this version is called the Su-34; with the name Su-25TK it is offered for export. The external appearance of new Su-25T differs from the old Su-25 due to the "hump" on the fuselage behind the cockpit and the large fairing (for the 192-tube chaff/flare dispenser) on the tailfin. Inside the aircraft there is new armament: the Shkval LLTV-system (*shkval* for squall) and the Mercuri FLIR pod, used for night attacks. (Dmitri Grinyuk)

Su-25T aircraft shown during the exposition for CIS leaders in Minsk, February 1992. Free-falling bombs and unguided S-24 missiles are seen in front of the aircraft. Under the wings, looking from the fuselage, you can see: Kh-29L heavy laser guided ASM, pack with eight "Vikhr" anti-tank missiles, an Kh-25ML laser guided ASM, B-13 rocket launcher containing five S-13 unguided rockets and an R-60 defensive AAM. (Dmitri Grinyuk)

Active infra-red jamming device in the tail of the Su-25T. (Piotr Butowski)

A Su-25K Frogfoot-A of the 30th Air Attack Regiment at Pardubice (Czecho-Slovakia). (Piotr Butowski)

A look into the cockpit of a Su-25TK. (Piotr Butowski)

A diving Su-25K. Note the dark trail of exhaust gas from Tumanski R-95Sh engines. (Piotr Butowski)

On 1 November 1989, three aircraft took-off from an experimental airfield in Saki, near the Black Sea. The aircraft flew a course towards the sea and the first Soviet aircraft in history to do so, besides the Yak-38 Forger VTOL aircraft, they landed on the deck of a warship. The first pilot who landed on the aircraft carrier Tbilisi was Victor Pugachov flying a shipborne Su-27K Flanker. After him was Toktar Aubakirov in a MiG-29K Fulcrum. The third aircraft was the Su-25UTG in the photo, piloted by Igor Votintsev and Alexandr Krutov. (Sukhoi Design Bureau)

The Su-25UTG (G stands for gak, or hook) with the side number 08 is the only airplane of this version; probably no more such aircraft will be made. It was used for testing take-off and landing techniques on aircraft carriers, and for the initial training of pilots. The photo shows the aircraft with its arresting hook lowered. The arresting hook is used for catching the braking cable when landing on board the aircraft carrier.

An anti-guerrilla version of Yakovlev Yak-52 training aircraft was produced in 1980, during the Afghan war. The aircraft was equipped with two underwing pylons and a simple sight in the cockpit. It could carry UB-32 unguided rocket launchers (see the photo) as well as gun containers and bombs. (Piotr Butowski)

The Blackjack flying majestically at low speed. Note the high-lift devices: protruded slots and double-slot rear flaps. The Tu-160 Blackjack is the newest aircraft of the former USSR. (Piotr Butowski)

A view inside the weapons bay. The basic armament of the Tu-160 are RK-55 (AS-15 Kent) cruise missiles suspended in two rotating magazines inside two bomb bays in the fuselage. Each magazine can contain six missiles. The missile is launched downwards from the magazine and then the missile engine is started. (Piotr Butowski)

In May 1987, the first Tu-160 came to the 184th Heavy Bomber Regiment in Priluki (Ukraine). Only this one unit is equipped with the Tu-160 Blackjacks. Twenty aircraft of this type were in service in 1991. (Piotr Butowski)

The cockpit of the Tu-160. Note the fighter-type control sticks and classical instruments. (Piotr Butowski)

The wing sweep angle set at 65° for fast flight. (Piotr Butowski)

Yugoslavia intends to make a multi-purpose aircraft Novi Avion. The design work has continued for 10 years. The expected speed of this fighter and fighter-bomber aircraft is Ma=1.8.

The Polish project PZL-230 Skorpion is designed for direct air support. The Skorpion will be fitted with two turboprop engines with pushing airscrews. The aircraft can carry 2,000kg of payload on eight pylons. The next Skorpion project, with two turbofan engines, is now under development.

A SABA class aircraft (Small Agile Battlefield Aircraft) was being designed by the Sukhoi Design Bureau and development is now continued by the newly established Russian Design Bureau of Yevgeni Grunin, a former Sukhoi deputy general designer. (Piotr Butowski)

In 1990, Sukhoi Design Bureau prepared a foredesign of the multi-purpose aircraft Su-37. The maximum speed will be Ma=2. It will carry 8,500kg of weapons on eighteen pylons. The Russians have suggested cooperation with Western companies and marketing to Third World markets. (Aerosvet)

1/144

AIR SUPERIORITY SERIES

4542 SU-27 NAVAL FLANKER 'TBILISI AIR WING'

4507 MIG-23MF FLOGGER B 'EAST GERMAN INTERCEPTOR'

4508 MIG-27 FLOGGER D 'SOVIET FIGHTER-BOMBER'

4509 SU-22M-4 FITTER K

4510 SU-22M-3 FITTER H

4514 MIG-29 FULCRUM 'SOVIET DOGFIGHTER'

4517 MI-24G HIND F 'SOVIET GUNSHIP'

4528 SU-27 FLANKER 'SOVIET INTERCEPTOR'

4531 MI-28 HAVOC 'SOVIET ATTACK HELICOPTER'

4539 MIG-27 FLOGGER J

PLASTIC MODEL KITS

1028 Military Aircraft of Eastern Europe: (1) Fighters & Interceptors
by Piotr Butowski

1024 After the Storm: Iraqi Wrecks and Fortifications
by Eric Micheletti

1026 Third Brave Rifles in the Storm
by Christopher Mrosko

1025 Merkava: Israel's Chariot of Fire
by Samuel M. Katz

2007 Sword in the Sand: U.S. Marines in the Gulf War
by Tony Engelhart & Pat Foran

2008 National Training Center: Ultimate in Land Warfare Training
by Greg Stewart

2009 Armor of the Afghanistan War
by Steven Zaloga, Wojciech Luczak & Barry Beldam

2010 The Balkans at War: Yugoslavia Divided 1991
by Eric Micheletti

2011 USAREUR: United States Army in Europe
by Michael Jerchel

4003 Final Touchdown: The Last Days of East German Air Power
by Hans Nijhuis